# The Late (As Usual) Bob Azurdia

## A Tribute

Roger Lyon

ISBN 0 9533414 0 2

Published by Roger Lyon

# FOREWORD

This is a happy book, all about a man who made everybody happy. So when I was asked to write this appreciation of Bob Azurdia I was delighted, because it allows me to pay my own tribute to a very special man.

As a presenter for Radio Merseyside, Bob interviewed me on numerous occasions. I treasure them still...those sessions of shared laughter, with Bob providing most of the jokes. With his beard and his stocky figure he looked like a larger-than-life mature Diddyman. He had a jolly booming laugh, a wonderful sense of humour and sometimes we laughed so much it was a wonder how we managed to pull ourselves together when the tape recorder began to roll. But we did. Bob was always the perfect professional.

We shared many things in common, notably a total unawareness of the passage of time. We both agreed that "time is an illusion". Yet in Bob's case I was somewhat amazed. Despite the fact that he was a very fit man who spent a great deal of his time running, he was never able to beat the clock. I remember the first time I met him. He'd arranged to see me at Radio Merseyside's Studio Five. "Where is Studio Five?" I asked the young lady behind the desk. "In the pub next door" she replied.

Potty on sport and a tireless worker for charity, Bob was blessed with a lovely wife and charming daughters. His legacy of warmth and good humour remains. If you can make a comedian laugh you're someone special. Bob was special. I feel happy just thinking of him.

**KEN DODD**

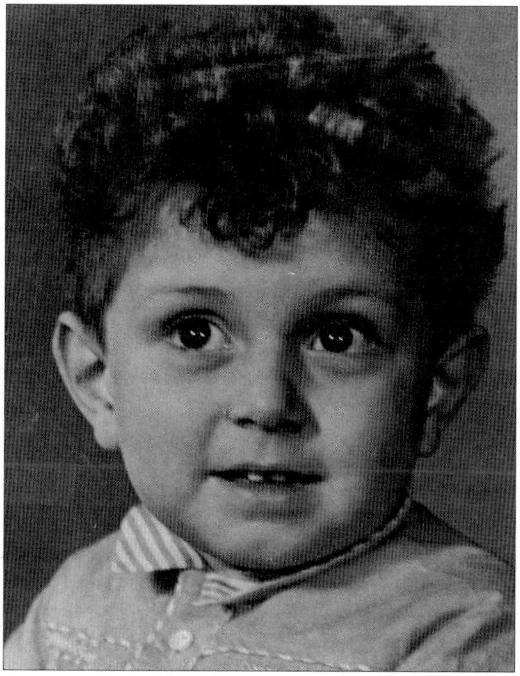

***A bright-eyed three year old Bob Azurdia***

Bob Azurdia was born on the 29th of June 1935 and died on the 21st of January 1996. Between those two dates was a life that was lived to the full and one that if told in its entirety, would fill a book that would make "War and Peace" look like a Monday night copy of the Liverpool Echo. One day, someone will sit down and write that book but, for my part, neither the time nor space is available. What follows therefore is not an attempt at Bob's biography. It is simply a few recollections of a man who made such a lasting impressing on just about everyone who met him and who, in the relatively short time that I knew him, came to be the best friend I ever had.

Bob was often asked about the derivation of his surname, which was not instantly recognisable as being of Anglo-Saxon origin. The family, on his father's side was originally from Guatemala which probably gave Bob his love of things Latin, although his mother's line of descent was in fact Irish, so that may also explain his passion for verbal communication.

Joseph Robert Azurdia, Bob's grandfather arrived in Liverpool in the early part of this century. He was a doctor by profession, but had been sent over by the Guatemalan Government to take up the post of Consul General and later went on to teach at the School of Tropical Medicine. He brought with him a large family but when, following a change of Government in Guatemala, he was recalled to his homeland, two of his children decided to stay in Liverpool. One was a daughter, Leonora, and the other a son, Robert. Robert inherited his father's interest in medicine, and studied to become a family GP. When he had qualified, he had surgeries in Rodney Street in the city centre and Park Road in Dingle.

Even today the name of Dr. Azurdia is recalled with great respect around South Liverpool. Robert also took over from his father as Honorary Consul General, but his domestic life was only settled when he met a lady called Josephine Kelly. Josephine was the daughter of a larger than life Irish immigrant, Joe Kelly and her union with Robert was productive. Three sons were born, Michael, who went on to follow the family tradition and became a doctor, Tony, who became a manager with Barclays Bank, and the eldest Joseph Peter Paul Robert, alias Bob.

Bob initially grew up in an affluent part of Liverpool 8 and attended La Sagesse Convent School. From there he progressed to St Edwards College where amongst other things he developed a love for Rugby Union Football. Eventually, more by accident than design, Bob entered Liverpool University to study Law.

He enjoyed his student days and found the social side of campus life very appealing, perhaps a little too appealing. He failed his final exams and was faced with having to earn his living outside of the legal profession. National Service saw him spend time in the Far East and he rose to the rank of sergeant before being demobbed. Bob considered his options and, deciding that journalism might be a good way to bring in the pennies, managed to land himself a job as a reporter with the Liverpool Weekly News. Once bitten by the journalistic bug, he took to it with great enthusiasm and he also ended up writing for the Widnes Weekly News, Melody Maker and Liverpool's own music paper, Merseybeat.

Through his work on Merseybeat and Melody Maker, Bob became friendly with many of the groups that made Liverpool such an exciting place in the 1960's. He was always being contacted by local musicians seeking publicity and, one day in July 1962, the telephone rang. As Bob recalled: "When the telephone rang and I heard a bright and breezy tone on the other end, my heart sank. You know how it is when you are in a position to help other people in one way or another. You get them all - all the hangers on, and Brian was a bit of a hanger-on! He'd tried a few things and had never been terribly successful in most of them but now he was branching into something new. "You must come over", he said. "Come over at once, they're the greatest thing since sliced bread. Come and have a listen."

***Launching the dummy announcing the start of the Catholic Pictorial in Liverpool (in December, 1961). On the immediate left is Norman Cresswell with Bob, the designated Chief Reporter, on the far right.***

I had nothing special to do at the time, so I went over and listened to the demo disc which he had in his office and I had to admit it was a pretty good number, particullarly the harmonica backing which I felt owed much to 'I Remember You', a Frank Ifield number which had topped the charts for eight weeks. I told Brian I thought it was likely to succeed. I then asked him about the band and I never forgot his answer. "They're going to be the biggest thing showbusiness has seen. They'll be bigger than Sinatra, bigger than Elvis, bigger than all those people put together. They're going to knock the world sideways!" I didn't believe him, of course but I promised to write about them in my column - which I did. It was, I believe, the first national publicity the Beatles received. I wonder whether Brian Epstein really believed that his words would be so prophetically true?"

In December 1961 Bob answered an advertisement for a reporter with a new local paper and the following month he began work on the Catholic Pictorial. The man who interviewed him for the position was the then Editor, Norman Cresswell. Norman recalls that one of the things which first impressed him about Bob was his politeness. Even after his appointment he always insisted on addressing Norman as Mr. Cresswell, and when ribbed about it by his colleagues, he revealed his reason for it. "It's quite simple," said Bob, "I can't go in and ask Norman for a rise, but I can certainly ask Mr. Cresswell for one!"

***Bob, the earnest reporter***

Around this time Bob was very much in touch with the young people of Merseyside, largely due to his work on Merseybeat and so when, in 1963, Norman Cresswell launched a new magazine called "Teenways", Bob was the natural choice as Editor. Norman was by now working for the BBC in Birmingham and often, after a long day, he would receive a visit from Bob, already a committed "nightbird", and would finish up pouring over the next week's plans for "Teenways" until four or five o'clock in the morning.

On many of these visits to the Midlands, Bob was accompanied by a young dark haired Italian girl who had recently entered his life.

Mariuccia Sebastiani first came to Liverpool in 1962 when she was here for a six month holiday. She was born in Carrara on the west coast of Italy and vividly remembers the contrast between her small sleepy hometown and the bustling vibrant metropolis that was Merseyside in the early 60's. Her family had had previous contacts with the Azurdias, but she had never before laid eyes on Bob. She knew that Bob was a regular churchgoer and she also knew that even then, he was not one to be out of bed at the crack of dawn. She discovered that Bob was in the habit of attending late morning Mass at St Phillip Neri Church in Liverpool 8 and so, one Sunday morning, not long before she was due to return to Italy, she went along to the service. Outside the church her eyes settled on him immediately.

He was rather difficult to miss, dressed as he was in a sage green corduroy jacket. Mariuccia was taken with him right away and remembers that he was "very cute with a passing resemblance to Clark Gable." It is rather doubtful that, in later years, many of his colleagues at Radio Merseyside would have made that connection but nevertheless, in 1962, to Mariuccia, he was suave, sophisticated and very much a prize catch. Contrary to Clark Gable however, Bob most certainly did give a damn, especially about this young Latin lovely.

Time was not on his side, as fairly soon after this first meeting, Mariuccia had to return to Italy. Undeterred however, Bob's response was to jump on a plane and follow her to Carrara, where he met her family and fell in love not only with Mariuccia, but with Italy as well. It was a love affair that was to last all his life and, of all the countries that he visited over the years, Italy was the one that he regarded as his second home.

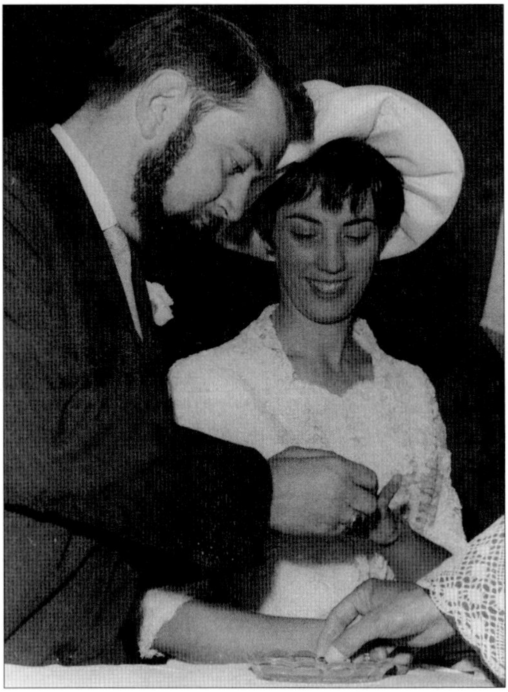

As far as Mariuccia was concerned, Bob was not about to let the grass grow under his feet. The day before he was due to fly back to Liverpool, he "informed" her that they ought to get married and that she had twenty four hours to make up her mind before the "offer" was withdrawn. Faced with this romantic ultimatum, Mariuccia decided that life with Bob had a certain appeal and was never likely to be mundane, so she accepted. They were married in Carrara on 3 September 1964 and settled back in Liverpool. In July the following year, their first daughter Suzy was born and then, in November 1969, Astrid completed the family.

Through the first three years of their marriage, Bob worked for the Catholic Pictorial but, in 1967, a new BBC Radio Station was due to open in Liverpool city centre. Mariuccia encouraged Bob to apply for one of the posts but the Bearded One

***Daughter Suzy's second birthday party***

wasn't too sure. He had a fairly secure position with the Pictorial and this new radio venture all seemed somewhat uncertain. Several times he decided to apply and several times he changed his mind until eventually the deadline for applications to be lodged was only one day away. This was cutting things fine, even for Bob. Fortunately Bob had a friend, Tony Horan, who already worked for the BBC in London and Bob rang him to ask if he could obtain an application form. Tony said that this wasn't a problem but getting it to Bob and then back to the BBC in 24 hours certainly was. There was only one solution. Tony Horan obtained the form, completed it on Bob's behalf and had it at the BBC with half an hour to spare to the deadline.

***Bob and Mariuccia on holiday at Carrara***

***Astrid celebrates her graduation with sister Suzy***

History relates that Bob's application was successful and the new Manager, Michael Hancock initially made him Head of Religious Programmes, although as the years unfolded, Bob was to be involved in just about every sort of programme that Radio Merseyside ever broadcast. It's an interesting thought that if Tony Horan had been half an hour later with Bob's application, this book may never have been written!

Michael Hancock, Radio Merseyside's first Manager, has vivid memories of his first meeting with Bob. It was in a room smelling of BBC linoleum in a daunting building known as 5 Portland Place, London, and the occasion was Bob's interview for the exciting new venture into radio broadcasting. Michael quickly decided that Bob's confidence and local journalistic experience was just what he was looking for. Bob was in fact "good boy makes local!"

Radio Merseyside went on air at 12

***Bob on a trial run before Radio Merseyside goes on air in November 1967.***

o'clock on November 22 1967, and started with an outside broadcast that was to welcome the listeners with a link up from land, air and sea. Fledgling presenters Victor Marmion and Jenny Collins were in the Mersey Tunnel, Gerry Harrison and Joyce Timewell were at the top of St. John's Beacon and Bob - well Bob was all at sea, literally. He was aboard the Royal Iris on the River Mersey. It all went swimmingly until it was time to cross to Bob. Fog had descended and completely obliterated his view of the waterfront and even Bob struggled to describe fog!

After the broadcast, Michael chided Bob about the fog, rather unfairly he now admits, but Bob had his response ready. He said "The last six months have made me a stranger in my own home, my beard's going grey already and now you are brow-beating me. But by God, it beats working!"

That was the start of Bob's 28 year love affair with the microphone and his thousands of listeners. His interests, enthusiasms and compassion knew no boundaries. Sadly, neither did his time-keeping.

In the late 60's, if you went up in the strangely puce coloured lift at Commerce House, you would have found "Azurdia's Army" in reception. There were clerics, sportsmen, politicians and various other itinerants, an eclectic mix that had one thing in common - they were all waiting for Bob. That was something that was constant throughout his entire career. The state of Bob's desk was also legendary. In the early days the BBC sent a trainer up from London to give the staff at Radio Merseyside some advice on their broadcasting techniques. He had a reputation for extreme tidiness and had, in fact, earned the nickname of Arthur "Clean as you go" Langford. After one session with Bob, he had to be escorted to his train at Lime Street station in tears, vowing never to return while "That man's mess covers every square inch of desk and floor space." Later that same night, Bob's desk mysteriously burst into flames, seemingly by spontaneous combustion and Radio Merseyside was lucky not to go off the air.

***A typical Radio Merseyside assignment interviewing workers in the Kingsway Tunnel***

There were very few people that Bob didn't get on with during his life. Sadly, the same could not be said for his many automobiles. Quite simply, Bob and cars were often a recipe for disaster. The main reasons for this were probably his insistence on purchasing the cheapest old bangers on four (and sometimes less) wheels, and then his indignation when they failed to perform as if they had just rolled off the assembly line in pristine condition.

One Friday night, in the early 60's, Bob decided to forsake his usual haunts such as the Blue Angel and the Jacaranda Club to go in search of a car. After a pint at Rigby's, in Dale Street, he decided to visit a second hand car dealer somewhere behind the Adelphi Hotel, dragging along with him John Sheperd, a colleague from the Catholic Pictorial. The Ribble Bus Station was then nearby, in Skelhorne Street, and the passing buses made getting at the motor of his choice very difficult. The cars were all housed in a showroom that was about the size of a superior garden shed and it so happened that the car that Bob had his eye on, was right at the

***Would you buy a used car from this man?***

back in the most inaccessible corner. It also transpired that the dealer had emptied all the petrol tanks and so, to get at Bob's car, all the others had to be pushed out into the street. This led to a quite alarming game of "dodge the bus" and Bob was visibly shaken when a large double decker missed his prospective pride and joy by inches. The car was a black Austin A40 Somerset with white piping, and although the bodywork had been well polished, it did little to disguise the rather overpowering smell of rodents! A test drive? Well, Bob would have been more than welcome to one, except that there was no petrol and besides, the car wasn't taxed. No matter, the car was cheap and Bob was going to have it!

Bob did indeed buy it and two days later he invited John Sheperd to accompany him to Swinton, where he was going to report on a football match for the Pictorial. John happily agreed to what he hoped would be a pleasant day out. Preparations were made. The L-Plates were taped onto the front and back and Bob got behind the wheel. He then donned his "driving suit", which consisted of a pair of circular lensed wire glasses. They were actually army issue eyesight correctors for the purposes of firing rifles on ranges and they gave him the look of a rather short-sighted Baldrick!

At the first press of the button, the starter motor jammed. Half an hour later, John Shepherd managed to unjam it but from thereon, it proceeded to whirr uselessly. Fortunately the car had come complete with a starting handle and, after a few lusty turns, the engine spluttered into life. It took only fifty yards for John to realise that if the car had indeed been fitted with shock absorbers, they had long ago ceased to be functional. Add to that the fact that Bob was still learning the rudiments of clutch control and the journey was, to say the least, taxing on their nether regions.

After what seemed like an eternity (to John anyway), the intrepid duo reached the Walkden section of the East Lancashire Road where for the umpteenth time, Bob stalled the engine. This time, however, the starter packed up again. John jumped out of the car brandishing the starting handle and began his vigorous efforts to spark the motor back to life. He had been winding the handle for a good ten minutes and had built up quite a sweat through his exertions when he suddenly became aware that, with every turn of the starting handle, he was taking a small step backwards in the direction of Manchester. Bob had left the car in gear! Had the engine fired, Bob would have been left with the task of explaining to his News Editor how a sports report had turned into a road accident story!

Over the years, Bob's automobiles came in many shapes and sizes. The common bond that they all shared was that they were old and falling to bits. One of the last cars that he owned was a very battered old third or fourth hand blue Yugo. Hardly a top of the range model. I was always aware that I was taking my life in my hands every time that Bob offered to give me a lift. The windscreen wipers hadn't worked for months, the windows refused to wind up or down and the heater blew out a continuous stream of ice cold air around the interior.

One occasion that has always stayed in my mind, was the night I accompanied Bob to Chester where he was due to record a chat with a visiting author for use on his programme "The Azurdia Interview". We managed to get about halfway when I felt the all too familiar "chug chug" of the engine giving up the ghost. We slowly ground to a halt and after numerous abortive attempts to revive it, Bob asked me if I could think of anything else to try. I replied that I couldn't but that I knew of a man who might. Half an hour later, the RAC patrolman arrived and after greeting Bob and myself, he slowly circled the Yugo, tutting and sadly shaking his head. He asked Bob what had happened to the other vehicle that had been involved in the accident, and looked absolutely incredulous when the bearded one replied that there had been no accident but that he had simply broken down. It took the RAC man nearly an hour to get us mobile again, although I can't remember precisely what the diagnosis of the problem was. Let's face it, it could have been any one of a hundred different things on that car, but nevertheless, Bob was pleased to be back behind the wheel again. At least he was until just before we pulled out to continue our journey. The patrolman signalled that he'd like a word and as Bob's window wouldn't wind down, he opened his door which creaked and groaned rather like that of a dungeon in the Tower of London. "Excuse me, sir" said the man from the RAC, "but have you ever considered selling your vehicle?" Bob replied in the negative, but wondered whether he had anyone in mind. "Well sir, my brother runs a scrap metal yard and I'm sure he'd give you at least £30".

Strangely for Bob, he failed to see the humour in that remark and, as we drove off, he ignored the smiling face of our rescuer who was left by the side of the road to contemplate just how long it might he before he was once again called out to assist Bob and his dilapidated useless Yugo!

"Do you run?"

"Only when I'm being chased", I replied with a failed attempt at instant wit. I turned towards the source of this rather peculiar question to find myself face to face with a man that I had never met before and yet one that I recognised immediately. He was a man of average height, slightly overweight and I guessed him to be in his early fifties. His appearance was "casual", dressed as he was in a white t-shirt and jeans, both of which seemed not to have come into contact with an iron for some considerable time. The features were kindly, with eyes that positively twinkled as they peered in a downward direction past the end of his nose and seemed to be viewing me with a mixture of curiosity and greeting. Under his arm, he held a collection of books and tapes that seemed to be about to slip from his grasp at any moment and, as my gaze settled on his trademark grey beard, I realised. This had to be Bob Azurdia.

It was May 1988, and I was sitting in the presenters office at BBC Radio Merseyside. I had always loved the medium of radio and had often dreamed of being able

***A surprisingly fresh looking Bob after completing the London Marathon in 1993***

to earn my living from it although, like so many other "wannabes", I had never seriously believed that I would get the chance. Now, suddenly, the chance had arrived and I was to be given the opportunity of presenting my own weekly programme called "In the Lyon's Den". I cannot claim any credit for the title as it was suggested by the then Manager of the station, the late and much lamented Ian Judson, and I had been a wage earner for long enough to realise that when you are a new boy, it pays to agree with the boss.

The office was open plan and, from my allocated desk, I could look around and see the spaces which were occupied on a daily basis by names and "voices" that had provided me, as a listener, with hours of great entertainment. Billy Butler, Wally Scott, Debi Jones, Roger Phillips and Alan Jackson were all people that I had tuned into and now here I was actually joining them. Bob Azurdia had been one of the original staff members of the station when it first opened in 1967, broadcasting from studios in Sir Thomas Street, and had over the next 21 years held more positions and carried out more tasks on it's behalf than anyone else could remember. In many ways he was "Mr. Radio Merseyside."

This was the man who, on this sunny spring evening, was enquiring about my possible athletic interests, although I had absolutely no way of knowing at the time that, over the next eight years, he would come to be, just about the best friend that I would ever have.

I introduced myself to him and we shook hands and I can remember being impressed by the warmth and sincerity of his welcome. He explained that one of his many sporting interests was running. He had in fact taken it up relatively late in life and had already completed several full marathons, many of them overseas.

Although I had always been a keen footballer and cricketer, my lack of enthusiasm for something as energetic as marathon running must have shown in my face but that wasn't going to deter Bob. "Well," he said, "the Liverpool Marathon is scheduled for September. You can run that with me".

That was it. He disappeared as quickly as he'd arrived leaving me to ponder whether or not he was actually serious and, if he was, how could I get out of it? During the following weeks, I convinced myself that Bob had in fact forgotten our initial conversation but, as September approached, I was brought back to reality when he casually announced that he had entered me for the race and there was no turning back. The story of that run is related later in this book but it turned out to be the first of dozens of races that I ran side by side with Bob - at least for a short while until he sped off ahead leaving me gasping for breath and wondering just why I ever let him talk me into it.

Bob could certainly be persuasive. It was one of his many qualities that left an instant impression on anyone who happened either by chance or design, to get into a conversation with him. Professionally, he was a first class interviewer who knew just how to put his "victims" at their ease and, while not afraid to ask the hard questions, always did so in a way that was disarming, yet friendly. He also possessed perhaps the greatest attribute required of an interviewer - he was a great listener. It didn't matter whether the questions were directed to someone from the political world, a writer, a sportsman or a showbusiness personality, Bob had a genuine interest in his subjects and it showed.

A social conversation with Bob, however, was another matter. Indeed, many of his friends would probably agree that it was virtually impossible to have a "conversation" with him. It usually took the form of a monologue. This was especially true whenever you were on the phone to him. You would realise that your audience with him was coming to an end when he would announce, "I'm going now because you are beginning to bore me". This would usually occur after he had been talking virtually non-stop for over half an hour and you had, on at least two occasions gently put the handpiece down, gone to the kitchen to make a cup of tea, and returned to find him still in full flow. Bob was never one for a few words when several would do!

The only notable exception to this rule occurred when Bob had in fact made the phone call himself and was actually having to pay for it. The conversation then could be fairly brief. Canny was a word that described Bob well!

There are, in fact, many words that could be used to describe Bob. Kind, compassionate, engaging, infuriating (at times), and most definitely LATE! Bob had a reputation for poor time-keeping that was extremely well deserved and one in which he seemed to rejoice.

The staff on reception at Radio Merseyside regularly had the task of assuring people who turned up to be interviewed by Bob their agreed time of arrival was cor-

*A rather smug Bob interviews Linda Lusardi*

*Frankie Laine takes over the microphone and is about to burst into song.*

*Two athletes, Bob and Jonathon Edwards. Jonathon appears to have beaten Bob this time although the triple jump was never Bob's favourite event.*

rect but that Bob had been "unavoidably held up" on his way in. The truth of the matter was that Bob was very much a night owl and, due to the fact that he consistently stayed up either working or watching old movies on TV until the early hours, it was rare indeed for him to be up in the morning unless there was a run or another sporting event taking place. Breakfast was normally taken at midday and he tried to avoid making any appointments before 2pm which, to Bob, was still the "crack of dawn". Over the years I developed a system whereby if I was arranging to meet him somewhere or other, I would tell him to be at the contact point at least half an hour before I intended arriving. I felt that there was then a reasonable chance of both of us rendezvousing at more or less the same time.

Perhaps if there was one word above all others that suitably described the Bob Azurdia that I knew, it would be "unique". He truly was a "one-off". He was a man who made a lasting impression on everyone who came into contact with him and, in a city such as Liverpool, which over the years has produced more than it's fair share of "characters", Bob will always remain up there with the best of them.

One Sunday morning in September 1988, I was standing in the middle of the road on Menlove Avenue in Woolton, surrounded by hundreds of people similarly attired to myself in shorts, singlets and running shoes. It was the day of the Mersey Marathon, twenty six and a bit miles of sheer torture. I remember being absolutely terrified. It wasn't the "bit" that bothered me, but the 26 miles had me wishing that I somehow managed to come up with an excuse to be somewhere else - anywhere else!

It was all Bob's fault of course. Some weeks earlier I had casually mentioned to him in the course of a conversation about his many running achievements, that I thought it must be a wonderful feeling to be able to say that you had completed a marathon. The next thing I knew, Bob had entered me for the Mersey and told me that it would be a "piece of cake" and that I would "stroll around" the course. He was so eloquently convincing that I decided that it wouldn't really need too much preparation and, in fact, the furthest that I ran in training was a mere six miles. Still, not to worry, Bob had promised to jog the race with me. He'd be with me every step of the way and, naturally, if I had to stop and rest at some point, he would wait with me. Why then, on this sunny Autumn morning, was I feeling that I would rather be at the dentist! It didn't take long for my fears to be realised.

The starting gun fired and the great mass of bodies slowly began walking, then shuffling and finally jogging forward. Bob turned to me and wished me luck - and that was the last I saw of him for the next 6 hours. He was away, like a scalded cat. As we made our way onto Mather Avenue, about one mile into the race, I thought just for a moment that I glimpsed the back of his green shorts a couple of hundred yards ahead of me, but as quickly as I spied him, he disappeared again in the main bulk of the field. It was at this point that I realised that I had been the victim of an Azurdia con trick - and it was too late to do anything about it.

My memories of this race, my first ever competitive event, let alone my first marathon, are still vivid. I recall every mile, every painful step of every mile and I remember thinking that if I actually survived the ordeal, then a certain veteran BBC broadcaster was going to pay dearly for my suffering.

It was a long day. Hours after the winners had collected their medals and gone home for a hot bath or retired to the pub for some well earned refreshment, I was still plodding up the Dock Road, through the Pier Head and on up through Otterspool, Aigburth and Garston, stopping at every opportunity that presented itself to

***An unchallenged Bob completes the 1992 Liverpool Marathon***

rest and accept sustenance from kind hearted Liverpudlians who, I concluded, could not possibly be spectators but more than likely workers on their way to clock on for the night shift!

The light was, after all, beginning to fade. As I eventually neared the finish at Camp Hill in Woolton, the thought struck me that possibly there would be nobody there to witness my great moment. In truth I wasn't too far wrong. After what had seemed like the worst six hours and eight minutes of my life, I finally staggered onto the field and faced the finish line. I strained my eyes (I'd already strained the rest of my body), to try and see if there was any sign of life and I managed to make out the forms of two officials holding stopwatches. A voice on the PA system announced my arrival, and enquired as to whether I realised that the moon had appeared before I had. I crossed the line with an amazing mixture of emotions, relief, joy, anger, elation and as I received my medal, I felt someone grab hold of my hand and start to pummel it up and down. "What kept you?" asked a voice that seemed rather familiar. I was too tired to answer, or argue, but as I surveyed the almost deserted finish area that had seen hundreds of runners and their supporters packing it during the previous three or four hours, I realised that one person had stayed just to greet me and congratulate me on my achievement. From that moment I knew that, though I would have to take my revenge on him at some time in the future, Bob and I would be lifelong friends from then on.

Bob and I ran together in dozens of races, ranging from tiny local charity 5ks to the splendid grandeur of the London Marathon and, yet, perhaps the event that I remember with most affection was one that neither of us actually ran in.

Bob had many admirable qualities and perhaps one of his greatest was compassion for his fellow man. He was always ready to offer help to anyone whose luck was on the wane. I remember that he was always the first to commiserate with me every time that I returned from seeing my Rugby League team, Runcorn Highfield, suffer yet another thrashing - and that happened pretty much every week.

I knew that Bob took an active interest in world events and often over a pint, he would hold court and relate in great detail the political and military conflict of a particular country and express deep feelings for the innocent people enduring the consequences. Nevertheless, he took me somewhat by surprise one day when, out of the blue, he suddenly informed me that he could no longer sit back and ignore the situation in Rwanda. Africa had always been a continent in turmoil. There always seemed to a famine in one country or another, but this was something extraordinary even by Africa's standards .

It was Sunday, 31 July 1994 and Bob and I had just finished a jog around his beloved Sefton Park. We were standing outside his house on the edge of the park and I was about to get into my car to drive home, when he asked if we could meet later that night. When I arrived at Radio Merseyside at the agreed time, I found Bob to already be there. This in itself was unusual, almost unique, because Bob was never normally on time for anything. He was about to make yet another phone call when I asked him what the urgency was all about. His reply was instant. "We've got to DO something. It's happening NOW". It turned out that Bob had been watching the television news reports the previous evening of the appalling scenes of starvation and misery in Rwanda and he had been affected by them so deeply that he had determined to try and do whatever he could to help. This was typical of the man and yet I was still somewhat surprised by the speed at which he was putting his plans into action.

Bob had decided that he would combine his desire to raise money for Rwanda with his love of running and that he would stage a fun-run in Sefton Park the following Sunday. Now, to the uninitiated, this may not seem to have been that great a task but anyone who has ever been involved in the organisation of a similar event, will understand only too well just what is involved. Road races, even small fun runs are normally planned and arranged months in advance. Bob was going to do it in just seven days. I naturally volunteered my help and in the week that followed, I came to realise just how many people Bob actually knew and, even more importantly, just how many people knew and liked Bob and were prepared to help him at the drop of a hat.

There were so many people to ring and visit and so little time to do it. Radio Merseyside gladly gave us access to the airwaves to publicise the event, and if their phone bill had seemed unusually large at the end of the week, they never complained. Fortunatcly, thcre was nothing else scheduled for Sefton Park the following Sunday, so the all clear was given. We next paid a visit to Steers House to ask favours of Bob's friends in the City Council's Leisure Directorate. Bob went straight to the top and we had a meeting with Norman Wilkinson, Head of Sport and Recreation Services, Judith Feather, Events Manager, and Ged Gibbons, Senior Events Officer. I suppose it helped that Bob and myself had always supported the Council's sports events in the past but they could not have been more co-operative, and I know how grateful Bob was for all their hard work. Not only did they agree to provide all the markers for laying out the course but they also donated the numbers for the runners' vests and even went so far as to arrange to deliver the Departments Events Caravan on the morning of the run for use as the registration area. The fire brigade were enlisted to help as was North West Water who provided a standpipe for refreshments. St. John Ambulance were persuaded by Bob's silver tongue to come along and give medical cover, and he even managed

***Another successful race. Bob with fellow runners Gerry Lindsey, Roger Lyon and Jim Callaway after the 1993 Speke 10k.***

to obtain some walkie-talkies from Raynet so that communications with officials around the course was instant

We also obtained a PA system which enabled us to inform everyone at the event exactly what was happening and to help create the very special atmosphere that existed on the day. The final requirement was a very human thing - bodies! We needed volunteers to act as marshalls on the course, people to take the registrations and hand out running numbers. People were needed as timekeepers and then to produce all the results. It is a testimony to the man that Bob had no difficulty at all in obtaining all the volunteers we needed and he even managed to persuade the then Lord Mayor, Councillor Roger Johnson, to come and officially start the event. The piece-de-resistance was the finding of a genuine Rwandan family who were temporarily living in Liverpool and Bob convinced them to come and actually take part in the run. All was now in place and our only concern was whether anyone would actually turn up to run.

Sunday, 7 August dawned, sunny and warm. It was only seven days since Bob had decided that he had to do something to help the poor people of Rwanda. Seven days in which dozens of phone calls had been made, several meetings taken place and countless favours called in, and now the day had arrived but would the people? We had been very careful not to advertise the event as a "Race" for fear of putting off anyone who had never taken part in such a run before.

Thanks to Radio Merseyside, and the Liverpool Echo and Daily Post, we advertised it as a gentle jog/walk around Sefton Park. The course was not too long, only about 5 kilometres but anyone who wished to be competitive was able to do so, whilst those who preferred a gentle saunter could also enjoy the morning.

I know that Bob was a little apprehensive as to the amount of support we would get, but in the end over 300 men, women and children and even a couple of dogs arrived to donate their £2's and participate in the Run for Rwanda. We provided everyone who finished with a certificate (again thanks to the Council) and when the takings were added to donations which arrived at Radio Merseyside, the final total was over £1,000. All this from a simple idea only one week earlier! Bob and I both acted as officials and MC's and so did not run ourselves but I think we both got as much satisfaction from the day as if we had just won the London Marathon. To me, that day will stay in my memory as a tribute to the people of Merseyside, and especially to Bob Azurdia.

Sport played a large part in Bob's life. Over the years he commentated on all the major sporting events on Merseyside as well as interviewing everybody who was anybody in both professional and amateur sport. He was also in attendance at all

***Run for Rwanda.***

the major international events including several Olympic Games where he reported for the Post and Echo and always made a point of seeking out Merseyside competitors for special interviews, no matter what their sport or performance.

An article Bob wrote in the 1960's perfectly sums up his attitude to sport.

"I must tell you about this little boy I saw on the bus yesterday. He was about ten and was wearing a very muddy football jersey under his school blazer. When I saw him sitting there, obviously very pleased with himself, I thought of another little boy - twenty years ago. This other youngster was rather plump, rather dull and rather shy. He didn't rate particularly with his schoolmates. In fact, he had rather an inferiority complex. This kid was, however, a great trier, an enthusiast! One day, early in September, they held trials at his school for the rugby team - and the unbellievable happened. The next day, when the school teams were posted on the noticeboard for the first matches of the season, there, amongst the fifteen members of the Junior Bantams was - MY NAME!

Yes, I was the little boy and I'll never forget my excitement. It seemed first of all to me that a mistake had been made, that my name had been entered in error. I don't know how I got through that week. I was in a permanent dream centered on the Saturday match. These dreams took the form of sporting fantasies. I would tackle and run ferociously. I'd score the winning try and then kick a goal for good measure. Somehow I was playing for the Junior Bantams at Twickenham and, miraculously, my team became England. Always I was playing in a vast stadium to roars of applause. Always I danced down the wing like an Obolensky or Jackson and we always won. Often or not, I WAS Jackson, Obolensky, Jeeps or Butterfield, though in fact I had been selected as a prop forward because of my weight. Somehow too, the game became a little confused. I found myself alongside Stanley Matthews at Wembley banging in goal after goal in the Cup Final. Then Billy Liddell and I defeated Everton together at Anfield and, along with Denis Compton and Cyril Washbrook, I brought the Ashes back from Australia and I knocked out Joe Louis to bring the Heavywight title back to Britain ....

Occasionally during this trance I had moments of panic. Suppose the match was rained off. Suppose I had an accident or there was a last minute change in the team. Suppose .... ANYTHING! Of course, nothing happened and the game took place as planned. We DID win. The score was 11-8 and, on reflection, I played a minor role in the victory. But that day, the whole week, left an indelible mark on me. I belonged. I had been chosen to represent, I had dignity, status and self-respect - and this was underlined when I was picked for the next match and, indeed, the whole season.

So I smiled when I saw the wide-eyed youngster on the bus. After my first game, I too had travelled home wearing a muddy jersey and football boots. I know what it means when you find you have "arrived" in schoolboy society. You want everyone to know. I got the message and rather envied him his brand new happiness."

Bob was also a great participator and was always ready to try his hand at something new. His was always the first name on the list whenever volunteers were

***Bob with Alan Parry live from the European Cup Final in Rome (1977)***

***Reporting from the Los Angeles Olympic in 1984***

required for the Radio Merseyside football and cricket teams. In football, Bob would usually either patrol the midfield area, or at least the centre circle, or alternatively he would position himself out on the wing, where he would regularly confuse full-backs by his deceptive lack of pace. Many an opponent would comment during the post match refreshments that Bob had somehow managed to be even slower than he looked. Nevertheless, nobody could ever question his enthusiasm and if that quality was all that counted, Bob would have made it to the Premier League. He also played his sport as he lived his life, in a gentlemanly fashion. He refused to commit fouls and considered it as a personal affront if anyone actually dared to prevent his progress by illegal means. I remember playing in goal for the Radio Merseyside team in a charity match at the Bebington Oval one day when a rather clumsy tackle landed Bob on the seat of his shorts. Before the resulting free kick could be taken, Bob picked himself up, dusted himself down, and turned to face his assailant.

With hands on hips and with his beard positively bristling with indignation, he glared at his opponent and said "Did you really have to do that? If you cannot display your skills without resorting to thuggery, might I suggest that you retire immediately and take up one of the Martial Arts". The poor man was so stunned that he immediately apologised profusely, promised to buy Bob a pint afterwards and, for the rest of the game, never ventured within ten yards of him.

Cricket, being regarded as the "Gentleman's Game", was perfectly suited to Bob, although he did at times adopt a somewhat strange approach to it. As well as playing for the Radio Merseyside XI, he also turned out from time to time for my Sunday team (Trinity Cavaliers) and quickly endeared himself to all the players. His popularity stemmed largely from his willingness to field in any position that was asked of him, even those that the rest of the team weren't keen on, such as those right next to the batsman. He also made a large impression on his team mates by his unorthodox fielding methods. For reasons only known to Bob, he categorically refused to stop the ball with his hands, preferring instead to use his legs and feet. This was Bob's technique no matter where he was fielding and no matter how hard the ball was hit in his direction. It was also a technique which quickly earned him the nickname of "Shins Azurdia", and one which usually left him with bruised legs that might have got him a part in 101 Dalmations.

It wasn't only his legs that Bob took risks with on the cricket field. If there was every any doubt that he was "blessed with a touch of eccentricity", that doubt was dispelled to anyone who ever saw him preparing to go out to bat. He usually agreed to don a pair of pads, (strange, considering his fielding), but gloves were always an optional extra that he often declined.

The one thing that he was steadfastly resolute about was that he would not wear a box. To the uninitiated, a box is a hard plastic piece of equipment which is designed to protect the most delicate parts of a batsman's anatomy but Bob, in true cavalier fashion, would not entertain one. Theories among his team mates as to why this was so were many and varied - and mostly unprintable. However, not even the possibility of becoming "soprano" would change Bob's mind. I did ask him once just why it was that he refused to wear a box. He replied "There is enough to worry about in life. Why should I worry about a little thing like that!" Enough said.

**A Grand Charity Football Match**

***************************************

**T.V. ENTERTAINERS XI**

including DAVE KING
ROBIN NEDWELL (Dr. Duncan Waring — "Doctor at Large")
BARRIE RUTTER (Douglas — "Queenies Castle")
MIKE McKENZIE and ROY HOLDER ("Ace of Wands")

VERSUS

**MERSEYSIDE ALL STARS XI**

including
BRIAN LABONE, ROGER HUNT, BOB AZURDIA

***************************************

**on Sunday, 5th November, 1972**

at SOUTH LIVERPOOL FOOTBALL CLUB

Kick-off 2-30 p.m. by Joe Royle

Gates open 1-30 p.m.

Free Car Park

**Admission by Programme 25p.**

All proceeds to be divided between the J.N.F. Charitable Trust and other charities

Billy Butler has a fund of memories of Bob, collected over many years. He played many times in the Radio Merseyside charity football team alongside Bob, and recalls how indignant Bob was that he should not be relegated to substitute, despite the availability of numerous former Liverpool and Everton stars. Bob took it as a personal affront and in fact categorically refused to wear the number twelve shirt. He also, typically for Bob, refused to spend money on items that he regarded as superfluous. These items included new football boots and, indeed, Bob's regular matchday footwear was a pair of boots that had probably been made when Stanley Matthews was a lad. They had the old cork studs, and had seen Bob through many a battle on muddy pitches across Merseyside. Unfortunately the years had taken their toll (on the boots, not Bob) and they had reached the stage were they had definitely seen better days.

Finally, during one game, Bob launched himself enthusiastically into a full blooded sliding tackle, only to find that as he made contact with both man and ball, both his boots completely disintegrated. He was faced with the awful truth, he would have to buy another pair. Billy, trying to be helpful, informed Bob that there was a sale on at Jack Sharps in Whitechapel, and that he would be able to pick up a good pair of boots for only £9.50. "NINE POUNDS, FIFTY" said Bob in horror, "My last pair cost me 30 shillings!" Nevertheless it was something that had to be done if Bob wished to continue displaying his soccer skills and so it was a reluctant Azurdia who opened his wallet and handed a crisp ten pound note over the counter at Jack Sharps. "For this money", said Bob "the boots should be gold plated".

The following Sunday Bob took the field resplendent in his new boots and was immediately involved in the action. The Radio Merseyside team were awarded a free kick just outside the opposition's penalty area and Bob placed the ball down and marched back ten yards in preparation for one of his blockbuster cannonball attempts on goal. The defensive wall was set and Bob started his run at the ball. The Azurdia right foot connected with full force and the ball ricocheted off the wall and went out of play for a corner. Billy, however, had noticed that Bob had collapsed and was rolling around on the floor, clutching his right foot and making pitiful noises which suggested he was in severe pain. "What's wrong, Bob?" enquired a sympathetic Butler.

"I think I've broken my foot" groaned Bob, "These new boots are useless."

He was helped from the pitch and after the match Billy again asked how he was feeling. In a voice that would have done credit to Victor Meldrew, Bob replied, "I don't believe it! These boots haven't got any steel toe caps!"

Billy tried to point out that steel toe caps had been obsolete in football boots since the days of lace-up case balls but Bob would have none of it.

"I paid £9.50 for these and they don't have steel toe caps. It's not good enough. I'm taking them back for a refund." And he did. The reply from the sales assistant at Jack Sharps when confronted by an irate Azurdia demanding his money back for a perfectly good pair of football boots is not recorded but the next time Bob took to the pitch for the Radio Merseyside team, his feet were enclosed in a pair of rugby boots - with reinforced toe caps.

One April day in 1992, Billy was sitting in the Radio Merseyside office when, through the door, trudged a very despondent looking Bob Azurdia. He wearily made his way to his desk, fell into his chair, and sighed deeply. Billy noticed that this wasn't Bob's usual demeanour, and wondered what was wrong. "Lost a fiver, Bob?" asked Billy.

Bob sighed again, took a deep breath and said, "William, there comes a time in every man's life when he has to face up to the harsh reality that the sands of time are slipping away, that the mountain he has been striving to climb, has in fact been conquered and that he is now on the way back down again. It is the time to accept that the capabilities of youth are now merely a distant memory and that whilst the spirit may still be willing, the body is now just a constant reminder of the limitations of mortality. That time came yesterday, William, at precisely 2.13pm when, whilst running in the London Marathon, and approaching Buckingham Palace, I was passed by the entire crew that rowed for Oxford University in the Boat Race."

Billy offered a kind word. "Surely that wasn't so bad, Bob," he said, "they must all have been young fit men. "

"Yes, " said Bob, "but they were carrying their boat!"

One thing that Bob and Billy had in common was their love of collecting and great reluctance to throw anything away. They both hoarded anything and everything but perhaps music was the main common denominator. The Azurdia and Butler households each contained vast numbers of records, singles, EP's, LP's and even 78's, and for many years Billy had been trying to persuade Bob to sell him his collection. Bob had always resisted these offers despite the fact that he rarely found time to play any of his platters, and had so many of them that he had no real idea of precisely how many there were. Nevertheless, Billy was persistent and from time to time would remind Bob that he was still interested in relieving him of them. One day, when they were both in the office together, Billy decided to try one more time.

"Hey Bob, you know all those records you've been going to sell to me for so long? Is there any chance I could come and have a look through them?"

"No."

"What do you mean NO?"

"I mean NO. I do not have them anymore."

Billy was nonplussed. "What's happened to them?"

"They've gone" said Bob, "I was burgled last night. Some (expletive) broke in last night while I was asleep and stole them."

Billy was amazed. "That's terrible, mate." he said "Weren't your alarmed?"

"Alarmed?" said Bob, "Alarmed? I was absolutely devastated!"

Charles Lambert is BBC's North West Sports Correspondent and has shared many sporting debates and more than a few pints with Bob over the years.

He remembers Bob as a man who invented the rules for broadcasting, and then proceeded to break most of them. As Charles recalls:

"Bob was famous, or infamous for his "flexible timekeeping." He would give fellow staff palpitations by cutting it fine when arriving for a live broadcast. Not even the threat of the sack, which was actually carried out on more than one occasion but totally ignored by Bob and eventually withdrawn, could persuade him to change his ways. The sight of Bob bursting into the studio, beard bristling with an armful of assorted tapes and records and just 30 seconds to go before he was due "on air" was not uncommon, and was responsible for many of his programme assistants turning prematurely grey. In a way Bob was a paradox. He seemed like a man who was uncommonly undisciplined and yet he was, in fact, someone who paid meticulous attention to detail."

Charles remembers one celebrated occasion when Bob had stayed at the station into the early hours editing a programme and, as he was due to present the Breakfast Show that morning, he decided it wasn't worth going home. He was discovered at 6am, fast asleep on the studio floor with a piece of cardboard suspended around his neck, on which was written, "Whoever finds me, please wake me up in time for my programme."

Charles says, "Exactly what his agenda was, only Bob knew. He accompanied Liverpool on a European trip to San Sebastian in Spain's Basque country but when the team and media arrived home, Bob wasn't among them. He'd had such a good time that he decided to stay and travel home in his own good time. The standing joke in the press box at both Goodison and Anfield was that the game couldn't start until Bob arrived! His penchant for living dangerously extended to his arrival for matches, when the sight of cables being furiously plugged in as kick -off time approached, became a familiar one.

***Duncan McKenzie selects the record while Bob looks on***

Events beyond even Bob's control took a hand in 1981 when he was in Paris to cover the Red's European Cup Final against Real Madrid. He was due to present his afternoon show live from the ground, only to be stymied when a mechanical digger sliced through the cables.

Bob was hurriedly re-routed to the BBC's Paris studio, where a surprised John Sergeant, now one of the Beeb's leading political correspondents helped him to get on air. A reporter who was due to fill substantial chunks of the programme was mugged on the street, but the show went on with Bob demonstrating his amazing ability to remain completely cool despite chaos around him."

There is no doubt that Bob was a true lover of sport and all it stands for. He was a firm believer in "fair play" and adhering to the rules. Charles recalls one occasion after Everton had played Wimbledon, a team known for its robust approach, when Bob could not contain himself. At the post match press conference, he demanded to know of the then Wimbledon manager, Bobby Gould, how he could defend the attitude of a team which was "a disgrace to English Football." Press conferences with football managers are not noted for such blunt questioning and many who were present expected the proceedings to be terminated forthwith. However, Bobby Gould invited Bob and the rest of the journalists into the dressing room, where, after lengthy debate, they agreed to differ, and parted the best of mates. Only Bob could have achieved that.

Neil Turner is a member of the Radio Merseyside sports team and was for many years a friend and fellow beer taster with Bob, often at the Greenhills Pub in Mossley Hill. He recalls a few years ago attending an Eve of Grand National Dinner with Bob and a few friends, at the Gladstone Hotel in Liverpool city centre. The entertainment was provided by top Liverpool comedian, John Martin and TV racing pundit Derek Thompson, so a good time was had by all. At the end of the evening Bob and Neil emerged from the festivities feeling distinctly "happy" to be confronted by a white carpet all the way up Lord Nelson Street to the hotel car park. Whilst they had been partaking of the hops and barley, snow had been falling steadily outside and was by now over an inch deep. Dressed as they were in lounge suits, they were hardly kitted out for winter weather and as they made their way gingerly to the hotel car park where Bob had left his clapped out old banger, they both had to take great care not to end up on the floor. The car park was approximately 100 yards from the hotel entrance but the conditions meant that it took them some moments to reach it. When they did, they realised that to raise the security barrier to get out of the car park, they required a token, and the tokens were to be obtained from the hotel reception desk!

"You wait here, Neil", said Bob as he turned and started slipping and sliding back in the direction from which they had just come, leaving Neil to stand alone in the cold snow covered parking area. Ten minutes later Bob was back having procured a token from the night porter. They both got into the car and Bob drove up to the barrier where he stopped and got out to insert the token. Unfortunately, a combination of best bitter, and sub zero temperature meant that the feeling in Bob's fingers was not all that it might have been and he dropped the token which promptly disappeared in the snow. Bob considered the situation. "I say, Neil, have you got a moment?" he said, and the pair of them spent the next five minutes on their hands and knees in the snow desperately trying to locate the missing token. Their efforts however were unsuccessful and eventually it was decided that the only course of action open to them was to go and get another token. Bob set off again to the hotel where he again encountered the night porter. Bob needed to be at his eloquently persuasive best to convince the porter of his plight, as the poor gentleman was worried that issuing more than one token was "more than his job was worth." Eventually, Bob managed to convince him that if he didn't supply him with a second token, then he would be unable to remove his car from the car park and get home.

Neil greeted Bob's return with relief as, by now, the cold was beginning to reach the parts that had only been partly numbed by alcohol. "Get in, my dear fellow" said Bob, as he inserted the token and watched the barrier rise. They both fastened their seat belts and Bob prepared to start the car. Unfortunately, as he tried to insert the ignition key, his cold fingers let him down again and he dropped it by his feet. His efforts to retrieve it were hindered by his seat belt which was pressing rather tightly on a stomach, already expanded by the copious amounts of food and drink that had been consumed earlier in the evening. As he frantically searched the car floor for the elusive key, both he and Neil became aware of the downward direction in which the barrier was moving!

As Bob approached the night porter's desk for the third time, the poor man viewed him with incredulity. "Are you trying to take the mickey out of me?" he demanded. His precise words were of a somewhat more robust nature but Bob, as always, retained his good humour and after much coercion, eventually managed to obtain a third token. Surely this time nothing could go wrong.

Bob trudged through the snow back to the car park where Neil was still waiting, by now almost rigid with cold. They both got into the car, fastened their seat-belts and Bob started the engine. It spluttered into life and Bob wound down his window, leaned out and inserted the token. The barrier once more rose and at last they were ready to move. Alas, it was not to be! After an evening of merrymaking, Bob's co-ordination was perhaps not quite what it might otherwise have been and, as he eased his foot off the clutch pedal, he stalled the engine. Despite frantic efforts to restart it, Bob's old jalopy refused to co-operate, and it was with feelings of utter disbelief that the dynamic duo watched the barrier lower itself for the third time.

Neil decided that he would accompany Bob back to the hotel reception which turned out to be a wise decision. The night porter was by now convinced that he was being set up and that Jeremy Beadle was about to make an appearance. It took some considerable time to convince him of what had actually happened and, in the end, he decided that the only way that he was going to be rid of these two nuisances was to take an active part in the proceedings. That was exactly what he did. He walked up to the car park with Bob and Neil, made sure they were in the car with the engine running before inserting the fourth token himself and at long, long last, Messrs. Azurdia and Turner were on their way home.

Another of Neil Turner's experiences with Bob involved the 1989 FA Cup Final between Liverpool and Everton. Naturally, being football fans they were both very keen to be at Wembley to witness the historic occasion, but with only a few days to go before the match, their prospects were not looking bright. Neither of them had managed to obtain a ticket and Neil had resigned himself to watching the game on TV when, only forty eight hours before the kick-off, his phone rang. It was Bob.

"Neil, old chap, great news". It was a happy sounding Azurdia. The previous evening Bob had met the proverbial "man in a pub" and had been made an "unrepeatable offer". As well as two match tickets, for only £7.50 each luxury coach travel with champagne breakfast would be provided. It sounded almost too good to be true! The coach was to leave Tuebrook at 7am on Saturday and Neil arranged to pick Bob up at his house at 6.30am. Needless to say, when Neil rang the doorbell, Bob was still in bed. Neil declined the offer of a cooked breakfast and after much cajoling, eventually shepherded Bob out of the house at 6.55am.

"Don't worry" said Bob, "They can't possibly leave without us. I've paid them £7.50. Bob was nothing if not confident. After a drive across Liverpool that would have done credit to Damon Hill, they eventually arrived to be greeted by Bob's "man in the pub". Significantly, there was no sign of the luxury coach.

Pleasantries were exchanged and everyone was looking forward to an exciting day. "Just one thing", said Neil, "when does the luxury coach arrive?"

"It's already here" said the man from the pub, and pointed to a vehicle parked a hundred yards up the road. Neil's gaze fixed upon an ancient Liverpool Corporation double-decker bus which had obviously seen better days. He turned to remonstrate with Bob but the bearded one was already walking towards the bus.

"Come on Neil, we don't want to be late!"

Neil took a deep breath and followed Bob as he boarded the "luxury coach" and climbed the stairs to the top deck. They settled into their seats and almost immediately the whole bus started to vibrate as the engine sparked into life. They were off to Wembley! They had only just turned out of Green Lane when their "champagne breakfast" was served to them by the steward who, Neil noticed, bore an uncanny resemblance to Bob's "man in the pub". The champagne actually turned out to be a glass of pomagne - but never mind, they were on their way to the FA Cup Final.

The bus had travelled no more than a mile and was just approaching the Rocket at Broadgreen, when Neil became aware that the engine was making some rather disturbing noises. As it gradually spluttered to a stop, he began to feel that perhaps he would have been better off declining Bob's offer and that he should have stayed at home and watched the game on TV. Half an hour later, after much muttering and tinkering of spanners by the driver, they were back on the road again. It proved to be an interesting journey. By the time they reached Birmingham they had had no less than six unscheduled stops for mechanical failure and even Bob was beginning to wonder if they'd make it to Wembley on time. Neil was doubtful that they'd make it at all!

It was during one of those stops that the two intrepid radio men struck up a conversation with the two people sitting in front of them. Both ladies were of somewhat indeterminate age, with bleached blonde hair, heavy make-up and were each carrying large canvas bags. Bob introduced Neil and himself, and enquired as to the ladies' names and professions.

"Yeh wha?" came the reply in a scouse accent so thick that it could almost have been cut with a knife. They turned out to be Cecile and Gloria, both from Kirkby.

"We're dancers" said Cecile.

"Really, my dear" said Bob. "Would that be ballroom or ballet?"

"Exotic" replied Gloria. "We're going down to London for some work". "Ah, and precisely what sort of work would that be?" asked Bob.

"You trying to be funny or wha?" said Cecile rather pointedly.

"Not at all my dear" said Bob as Neil tried desperately not to let the ladies notice his smile. Bob commented on the large canvas bags and was informed that they contained the ladies' stage props.

"Would you like to see?" said Cecile as she picked up her bag, opened the top and passed it back over the seat onto Bob's lap. Bob and Neil peered down into the bottom of the bag and visibly blanched.

There, curled up in the corner was an extremely large python, which Cecile used in her act. Bob decided not to enquire too closely as to precisely how Cecile used the snake and contented himself with "Ah yes, very nice", before quickly passing the bag back to the front seat where Cecile placed it back on the floor.

The next hour was relatively uneventful as the bus trundled south and both Bob and Neil managed a gentle snooze. Suddenly the peaceful air was broken by Cecile's voice, "Oh my God, it's gone". The python had escaped. After frantic scrambling underneath the seats had failed to locate the missing reptile, Bob took charge of the situation. He stood in the centre aisle and addressed his fellow passengers.

"Good morning, ladies and gentlemen. I do hope that you are all enjoying your journey on what is undoubtedly a wonderful day for all football fans on Merseyside. I know that we have had one or two small problems on the way but I trust that you will not let them spoil your enjoyment of a truly grandiose and historic occasion."

He paused. "By the way - has anybody found a snake?"

After the ensuing bedlam and mayhem had subsided, the python was finally located and returned to a grateful Cecile. The bus arrived at Wembley with minutes to spare and Neil and Bob got to see the match.

The return journey was made without Cecile and Gloria, who had found a couple of "friends" and were last seen downing several gin and tonics in a local hostelry. The day had an unfortunate end for Neil Turner. He had promised his wife that he would be home by nine o'clock in order to have a night out with some of his relations who were visiting from Canada. Unfortunately the bus suffered another major breakdown which resulted in a delay of several hours, during which Bob and he sought refuge in a Birmingham pub. Having finally arrived back in Liverpool well after midnight in a condition that could have been described as "well oiled" it took several days before normal relations were restored in the Turner household. Bob, however, had had a good day!

Marcus Buckland (aka Blewett) was a member of Radio Merseyside's sports team in the early 90's before moving on to work for Radio 5 Live and Sky Sports TV. He has vivid memories of Bob.

"The bristling beard, those mischievous eyes and the deliberate pause before answering a question - that's how I remember Bob Azurdia. He always made me laugh, intentionally most of the time, and his delightful eccentricities still bring a smile to my face. Time meant nothing to him and more than once he collared me as I was en route to read a sports bulletin and launched into some never-ending yarn which I'd listen to with increasing desperation as the clock ticked by.

Once in conversation, he seemed to forget about everything else. An example of that occurred in the middle of one of his programmes. Having put on a record, he dashed out of the studio to collect some more discs from the record library. On his way back, he met somebody and became so deeply embroiled in a discussion about nothing in particular that he completely forgot about his programme. He was only reminded of it when a senior manager suddenly appeared and suggested to Bob, that as his last record had finished more than two minutes ago, his audience were unlikely to be entertained by the "dead air" (silence) that was presently being transmitted!

Bill Shankly was one of his more formidable sparring partners. At one post match

press conference the Great Man looked Bob firmly in the eye and said "I've been asked a lot of stupid questions during my time in football, Bob, and you've asked most of them!

At one stage Shanks even banned Bob from his press interviews but undeterred, our hero invested in an extra-long microphone lead. As all the scribes jostled around the Liverpool manager for a quote following another great Reds performance at Anfield, a microphone suddenly emerged through the crowd and gradually began to rise from the floor until it was hovering inches from Shanks' mouth. A deathly hush fell on the entire room and as the massed ranks of reporters parted, rather like Moses and the Red Sea, there was Bob, on his hands and knees looking more than a little sheepish.

I arrived on Merseyside in 1989 and, by the time I left in 1992, I'm proud to say that Bob had become a good friend. He somehow persuaded me, (with the dubious assistance of Roger Lyon, and against all my better instincts) to take up jogging and I competed in several races culminating in the 1993 London Marathon. I'll probably never forgive him for the agony that caused me, but I must say that he was always good company during these runs,  moreso in the bar after them! He was also great fun at football matches with his witty, cynical comments, not to mention his considerable knowledge. Whenever I travel back to Merseyside, memories of Bob flood my mind and the press boxes at Anfield, Goodison and Prenton Park are much the poorer for his absence."

Many stories about Bob have been passed down over the years and told and retold in radio studios, football grounds and pubs all over Merseyside. As with all tales that are transferred by word of mouth, there is a tendency for bits to be added, exaggerated or left out altogether. However, in the case of J.P.P.R. Azurdia, I feel that most anecdotes concerning him have remained fairly constant and factual.

A few years ago, Bob was due to attend a black tie sports presentation evening organised by the Liverpool Echo. As always, he had pottered through the day in his normal haphazard way and had been late for all his appointments. Time, which meant nothing to Bob, soon passed, and almost before he realised, it was time to get ready. The function included a dinner and was to be attended by all the great and good from the world of sport. Bob was to be one of the honoured guests and was to present some of the awards. Ten minutes before the dinner was due to start, he was still ensconced in Studio 3 at Radio Merseyside, editing tapes of one of his forthcoming programmes. This was of no real concern to Bob because after all, surely they couldn't start without him. Still, it was probably time to get ready, so he left the studio and went upstairs to the office to get changed. Off came the t-shirt and jeans which were Bob's standard attire and on went his smart dinner suit with black dicky bow. He viewed himself in the mirror and decided that he cut a fine figure. There was, however, just one small problem. He had forgotten to pack his shoes! He checked and re-checked his bag but his patent leather black shoes were nowhere to be seen. All he had was the scruffy ancient pair of battered trainers in which he stood.

Urgent action was required but there was no time to return home. There was only one thing for it. Bob began a quick tour of the building accosting each and every male member of staff that he came across. Unfortunately, as it was evening time, members of staff, male or female were rather thin on the ground. Nevertheless, Bob was undeterred and various reporters were approached in the newsroom as well as a couple of members of the sports department. All to no avail. Nobody had a pair of shoes that matched Bob's size. His only remaining hope was Wally

Scott, who was working late in the upstairs office, but small as Bob's feet were, Wally's were even smaller. Wally enquired as to what Bob planned to do, fully expecting him to announce either that he would return home for his shoes or cancel the evening altogether. Bob was having none of that and everyone who attended the city centre hotel that evening for the dinner was greeted with the sight of Azurdia at the top table resplendent in his dress suit, and his feet looking as if he had just completed a run round Sefton Park!

Bob was always a great traveller and over the years he visited many countries, sometimes to take part in marathons and other times simply as a tourist. He would think nothing of simply taking off to far flung corners at the drop of a hat, just because he'd had an idea that it "might be fun." One such trip occurred back in the early 60's before Bob had been introduced to the radio microphone. He had been hitchhiking across Europe armed only with a backpack and had decided to take in some of the Eastern bloc, which in the days of the cold war was easier said than done.

After much criss-crossing of border check points, he finally arrived in the Bulgarian capital of Sofia, at a time that coincided with a State visit by the then soviet leader, Nikita Kruschev. This was too good an opportunity to miss for Bob and he was grateful that despite losing many of his personal effects such as combs and toothbrushes during the previous fortnight, he had still managed to retain his most treasured possession, his press card.

He resolved to try for the scoop of the year by interviewing the Russian Premier and headed directly for Sofia's top city centre hotel where Kruschev was due to attend an official welcoming function. Brandishing his precious press card, Bob somehow bluffed and blustered his way through a myriad of security guards and Bulgarian police and eventually found himself amid a throng of dignitaries and journalists who were all waiting to meet the man who was effectively the leader of Eastern Europe. In those days, Bob already sported his trademark beard but then it was completely black with no trace of the grey which appeared later. He was, as chance would have it, also wearing a black peaked hat and as Krushev entered the hotel lobby, his eyes fixed on Bob. Nikita's face lit up and he marched straight up to a startled Azurdia with open arms. Bob was embraced and kissed on both cheeks by the delighted Russian, who had mistakenly thought that he was the Cuban Communist leader, Fidel Castro.

"Cubanski Cubanski" roared Kruschev.

"Er, Actually no" said a sheepish Bob, "The Catholic Pictorial, Liverpool."

The day before his untimely death, Bob was at Anfield to watch the Reds take on their old Yorkshire rivals, Leeds United. Leeds included in their line-up, their recent £4 million Scandinavian signing, Thomas Brolin, but on the day he did not have the happiest of games. To put it mildly, he was not very involved in the proceedings and, when one of Bob's colleagues in the press box asked the bearded one whether he was impressed that the Premier League now included a player from the Arctic Circle, Bob's reply was immediate.

"I don't know about the Arctic Circle," he said. "I've not seen Brolin move out of the centre circle all day!"

Then there was the time when Bob was holidaying in Morocco. He had been wandering around the country somewhat nomadically when, by sheer chance, he arrived in Marrakesh just as the Moroccan marathon was about to take place. Unable to resist the temptation to add another medal to his collection, Bob decided to enter. The race began at 6pm to avoid the heat of the day and Bob noticed that the field was made up almost exclusively of locals who were viewing the pale-skinned bearded foreigner with a mixture of amusement and curiosity. It only took a few miles for Bob to realise that he may have made a mistake. He had quickly become detached from the rest of the runners who had sped off ahead and he faced the prospect of a further twenty plus miles running alone.

Bob had been used to running mainly large city marathons through urban surroundings but this was something entirely different. Most of the course passed through what could almost be described as desert with very few landmarks to take bearings, save several large sand dunes. There was also a marked lack of marshalls to direct the runners on the right path and eventually, with the light rapidly fading, Bob shuffled to a halt, and came to the conclusion that he was in fact lost. This was a worrying predicament but not one to defeat our hero.

He continued trudging through the sand guided only by the light from the stars, and, after a mile or so, he realised he was not alone. Standing in front of him in flowing Arabian robes was a man with a camel. It was quite a shock for Bob but, I suspect, an even bigger one for the Arab, and certainly for the camel. Despite the fact that neither spoke the other's language, communication was established, proving yet again that Bob could talk to absolutely anybody. The camel driver accompanied Bob back to the marathon course and, eventually, just before midnight, a tired and relieved Azurdia reached the finish line. Unfortunately, by the time Bob arrived, everyone else including all the officials had left. The organisation was not quite the same as Bob had encountered in London and New York but, nevertheless, he had completed the course and, even if he had finished plum last, he had earned his medal. The trouble was that there was nobody there to give it to him.

It took him almost two hours of visiting almost every hotel within a mile radius (just what you need after running 26 miles) before he finally tracked down the race organisers. They were astonished to see Bob, as they believed he had dropped out of the race early on. Profuse apologies were offered along with invitations to return the following year as a guest of honour, an invitation that was graciously accepted a few years later. It was an exhausted Azurdia who finally collapsed into bed at 5am, just as the sun was appearing on the desert horizon. He was footsore but happy. Bob had got his medal, thanks to a man and a camel!

My memories of Bob seem almost infinite. Several times we ran up the stairs of the Liver Building, from basement to roof on Children In Need Day, as part of the Radio Merseyside team. This was actually an event that Bob originally thought up and one which has raised hundreds of pounds for the charity over the years.

I remember one time when, after accompanying Bob on a tour of the city centre back street pubs, he decided he wanted to go for a meal. Bob was a notoriously slow eater. He would take his mother's advice to "chew your food properly", to extremes, and after I had worked my way through, soup, special fried rice and banana fritter, Bob was still sitting opposite me, slowly masticating his prawn cocktail starter. After I had waited a further two hours for him to finish his three courses, I was almost hungry enough to order again. I vowed to myself that I would never again visit a restaurant with him.

It was 8.30am on Monday 22nd January 1996 and the ringing of the phone roused me from a fitful sleep. I'd been back in Australia for only ten days after spending a three month break back in Liverpool and was just getting over the final remnants of jet lag. I picked up the phone, still trying to force my eyes to stay open and immediately recognised the voice on the other end of the line. It was Maureen

Walsh who, as well as being a good friend, had previously been my producer on the afternoon programme. I was delighted to hear from her but what she had to say instantly awoke me and shook me to the core.

***Bob with Roger Lyon after completing the annual run to the top of the Liver Building to raise money for Children in Need***

Maureen had wanted me to hear the news first from her - Bob Azurdia was dead. It took several seconds for the news to sink in and several more before I could bring myself to ask about the details. Bob had been suffering with a cold for a couple of weeks but typically had decided on Sunday 21st to go and run in the Four Villages half marathon at Helsby. It had been a bitterly cold day but Bob had soldiered on and completed the course, seemingly with no more than the usual aches and strains which you would associate with a thirteen mile run. However, half an hour after crossing the finish line, he began to complain of chest pains and collapsed. An ambulance was called but by the time it reached the Countess of Chester Hospital, it was apparent that Bob had, sadly, run his last race.

Many thoughts flashed through my mind as I struggled to find words for Maureen. She apologised for being the bearer of such bad news and then had to hang up as she was due to present the late show that night on Radio Merseyside. (It was still Sunday night in England). As I replaced the handpiece, I was engulfed in stunned disbelief. Surely Bob couldn't be dead. He'd always seemed to be someone who would live indefinitely. He was a part of the furniture.

Slowly the reality of it began to sink in and I pondered on the events of the previous three months. I was glad I'd been able to spend so much time with him. We'd run several races together and also enjoyed many jogs around his beloved Sefton Park and also along the waterfront to the Britannia Pub and back to Radio Merseyside. I recalled the evening that Bob and I were sitting in Radio Merseyside reception after just such a run, when Wally Scott came down the stairs on his way home. I could see the look of apprehension in Wally's eyes as Bob engaged him in conversation. Once Bob started talking it was almost impossible to get away and I could tell that Wally had visions of still being there at midnight.

The talk inevitably turned to sport and Bob enquired whether Wally had ever considered taking up jogging. This was where Wally made his mistake. He replied that he needed to do something to get fit and maybe, just maybe, jogging was the answer. Bob was in like a flash and in ten minutes flat had poor Wally lined up for the next London Marathon. The look of relief on Wally's face when he finally managed to escape was a picture. In retrospect, I think that Bob was probably wasting his time trying to get Wally to take up jogging. It would have been murder on his hair!

One Sunday just before Christmas, Bob had asked me to do him a favour. He was attending a rather well-to-do party in Woolton, and anticipating that he would be consuming a fair amount of alcohol, he asked if I would pick him up and drive him home. I arrived as arranged at 11pm at a large house on top of Woolton Hill which was festooned with fairy lights and from which came the sounds of some serious merrymaking. The driveway to the house and the road were filled with Bentley's, Jaguars and Daimlers and, as I pulled up in my battered old Astra, I did feel somewhat conspicuous. Nevertheless, I was looking forward to sampling the abundant refreshments which Bob had promised to save for me and so I strode up to the large front door and knocked. As the door opened the sound of music and laughter hit me full in the face and I looked up to see a somewhat intoxicated figure in a shimmering sequinned dress (no, it wasn't Bob!) peering out at me with a rather disdainful look.

"Yes" she said in a voice that was so far back it was almost horizontal, "Can I help you?"

"I've come to pick up Bob Azurdia," I replied.

"Wait there" she said, and as she closed the door, I heard her call out, "Taxi for Mr. Azurdia."

A minute later the door opened again and the sequinned dress informed me that Mr. Azurdia would be out in due course and that I was to wait for him. Before I could tell her that I was not a taxi driver but rather a personal friend, she was gone and the door again closed.

I may have omitted to mention that being December, Liverpool was not exactly in the throes of a heatwave and I could clearly see frost on the roof and pavement. Not only could I see it but I could feel it as well, it was freezing! I waited - and waited, and twenty minutes later, I was still waiting. I was contemplating the possibility of hypothermia when the door again opened and there stood the sequinned dress.

"Mr. Azurdia thought you might like something to warm you up", she said, and handed me a packet of extra strong mints! Rarely has a friendship been so sorely tested and when, ten minutes later, the bearded one finally appeared, his eyes positively twinkled as he enquired of me - "Have you been waiting long?"

My reply cannot be printed on these pages but suffice to say it was brief and to the point. Bob laughed, wished me a Merry Christmas and despite his somewhat "merry" state, instructed me to drive him to Paradise Street where we spent the next two hours producing jingles for my forthcoming programmes.

I remembered the night that we'd been in the studio until 11.30pm and then bumped into Ken Dodd who had been doing an interview for Radio 2. Now Doddy, as everyone knows, is not a man who is usually lost for words, so a conversation between Messrs. Dodd and Azurdia was one of epic proportions. I did think at one point that we might all end up in Richie's butty bar for breakfast but, eventually, Ken presented us with tickling sticks, and headed off down Paradise Street. Bob was left regretting that he hadn't recorded it all for use on a future programme, but I doubt that there would have been enough tape available in the studio!

Christmas and New Year 1995 were special times. I had never been a regular church goer but Bob always attended the Midnight Service on Christmas Eve and that year he asked me if I'd like to go along. In the light of subsequent events, I was glad that I did, and it was certainly a very moving service. On New Year's Eve I called round to see Bob and Mariuccia and distinguished myself by knocking over their Christmas tree and consequently the lounge carpet was almost completely covered in pine needles. Each time I tried to stand the tree back up, the base would collapse and over it would go. This happened at least six times and each time the pile of pine needles would grow higher and higher. It developed into a scene reminiscent of a Laurel and Hardy comedy and ended in all three of us collapsed in heaps of hysterical laughter.

Perhaps my most poignant memory of these times was what turned out to be the last time I ever spoke to Bob. It was Wednesday, 10 January 1996, and I was at home waiting for a taxi to take me to the station as I was travelling back to Australia. Just as the taxi arrived, the phone rang and it was Bob. We chatted briefly and he wished me luck. His final words to me were "Have a safe journey - you'll be missed." Little could either of us have known that in less than a fortnight, it would be Bob who was being missed by everybody who knew him!

In the days that followed Maureen Walsh's call, I also received calls from Angela Heslop, Linda McDermott and Eunice Wise which I was very appreciative of. It was very difficult and frustrating to be so far away at a time when I felt I should have

***Relaxing at home with Mariuccia***

been here offering any help that I could to Mariuccia and Bob's daughters.

I was unable to attend either the funeral or the Memorial Service which was held in the Metropolitan Cathedral although I did get first hand reports of both. The one consolation that I derived from it all was the number of tributes that poured in from people of all walks of life. Bob was a man who rarely, if ever, had a nasty word to say about anybody, and in the eight years that I was privileged to call him my friend, I honestly never heard anyone say a bad word about him. That is probably the greatest epitaph I can give him.

Bob was buried in a family plot at St. Austin's Church on Aigburth Road alongside his mother and father. Mariucca has had a headstone erected with words that she took from Ken Dodd's tribute at the Memorial Service - "You touched so many lives."

# POSTSCRIPT

## SYDNEY - SEPTEMBER 1996

Eight months after Bob's death, I was still living in Australia and I was fortunate to obtain a couple of tickets for the Rugby League Grand Final which was to be held on 29 September at the Sydney Football Stadium between Manly and St. George. I travelled down to Sydney with a friend, Brian Bell, a fellow scouser who also lived in Newcastle, NSW, anticipating an exciting day. So it proved.

The stadium was full to capacity and the rugby was enthralling, keeping everyone on the edge of their seats. The pre-match and half time entertainment was as spectacular as only Australia seem able to stage, and in fact the only thing which seemed determined to dampen a marvellous day was the weather. High winds swirled around the stadium and dark billowing clouds brought long periods of steady rain. The game ebbed and flowed but at the final whistle Manly were victorious by 20 points to 8. The players lined up for the presentation of the Cup and Brian and I made our way from our seats at the back of the stand down toward the exit. As we reached pitch level, the tannoy was blasting out Tina Turner "Simply the Best" which is the theme song for the Australian Rugby League. We were about to leave the ground when the players began their "lap of honour" with the cup, and as we were now right next to the pitch, I suggested to Brian that we should stay for a moment to see them go past at close quarters. We were virtually within touching distance as the Manly team neared us, and the cheering thousands that surrounded us made the atmosphere electric.

I turned to Brian and commented that my old friend Bob Azurdia, who had always loved the big sporting occasion, would have given anything to have been there on this day and, indeed, I also would have given anything for him to have been there. What happened next made the hairs on the back of my neck stand on end!

The moment that I mentioned Bob's name, the rain stopped and a bright ray of sunshine broke through the clouds overhead, instantly lighting up the part of the pitch in front of us. The strangest thing though was that Tina Turner faded from the PA system and in her place a song began that seemed to have little or no relevance to the occasion. It was Louis Armstrong's "What a Wonderful World" . Now this is a lovely song but not one that you would normally associate with Rugby League Grand Finals. It was however, Bob's all time favourite record and one that was played at both his funeral and his Memorial Service.

Perhaps it was just coincidence. Maybe I read too much into it, but as I recovered my composure and made my way back to Sydney Central railway station, I felt very comforted to think that Bob may as always have been "late" but at least he'd made it to the match!

### AND FINALLY

Some recollections of former colleagues, friends and listeners.

"Bob Azurdia was one of the most talented presenters Merseyside has ever produced and he left a distinct impression with anyone he came into contact with. He was particularly keen to give encouragement to young journalists and his advice on interviewing style was always first class. Even now, more than two years after his death, his name is mentioned daily at Radio Merseyside. His impact will be felt for many years to come.

It is a real shame that he is no longer here to influence and befriend a new generation of broadcasters but, thankfully, his legacy is still with us among the many hundreds of hours of tapes he has left, some of which Radio Merseyside is planning to broadcast in the coming year.

Whilst there have been many changes at Radio Merseyside over the years, it is important that we recognise the real tradition we inherit; Bob Azurdia did more than most to shape that tradition and his place is assured in the Station's heritage."

**Mick Ord (Editor) BBC Radio Merseyside.**

Bob was always excellent company. True his eccentricity and a lack of urgency could frustrate - especially if you were trying to get a programme on air, or catch a train, but you always forgave him because Bob was such a warm, amusing and engaging colleague and friend.

**Eric Wise (Senior Producer) BBC Radio Merseyside.**

I first met Bob Azurdia in 1975 when I joined BBC Radio Merseyside as a part time production secretary. Bob - as he always did with new people took me under his wing and asked me if I'd like to help him with his quiz recordings. My first introduction to the world of broadcasting! I kept score and, like everyone, hated the sound of my voice!

However, the sting in the tale is that after the recording in the studio in Sir Thomas Street, we'd always end up in a local hostelry, enthralling the assembled group of quiz teams and helpers with stories of interviews with Krushchev, the Pope - and almost every other famous person you can mention.

Bob's left a permanent legacy of his (almost) three decades with the Station and, one day, we'll broadcast them again. A real treat in store!

**Ev Draper (Assistant Editor) BBC Radio Merseyside**

***Interviewing John Smith.***

Bob was a real observer of the human condition. I never heard him speak ill of any person. He had a wry wit and an elephantine memory. They never "broke the mould" when he was born, he kept it with him and, I suspect, took it with him when he went. Buona Nothe Commendatore Azurdia.

**Brian Jacques (Presenter) BBC Radio Merseyside.**

My friend Ivy Clark and I always went along to the Liverpool marathons, mainly to cheer on my son-in-law but we never went home until we had given Bob Azurdia the loudest cheer of all, even if it meant that we were there at the roadside by the old Speke Airport for three or four hours waiting for him. He was worth it.

**Muriel Hammond, Garston (a listener).**

I had a dance with Bob when he was our rep on one of the Radio Merseyside holidays to Bournemouth. He was lovely.

**Emily Cross, Cressington (a listener).**

When I went to Liverpool University in October 1957, Bob was already there. Many years later, after working abroad, I returned to hear Bob's voice on the radio. The Azurdia Interview series was so skilfully prepared and so well done, that one was not aware of the hard work behind the scenes. Bob's enthusiasm and encouragement remain as a good and helpful memory. I wish to pay tribute to the undoubted benefit his life has been to so many, whom he did not even meet, but who are richer for having heard him.

**Susan Nicholson, Bromborough (a listener).**

Two men played a very big part in my career at Radio Merseyside and indeed in my life. Both men sadly, are no longer with us. The first was Ian Judson a friend and former station manager. Bob was the other. I talked to Bob about problems at home and work, he listened intently always, whether the problem was a very small one or in my mind, a very large one. His wise words, the twinkle in his eye and on occasion, big hug dissolved any problem - he helped remind me of the really important things in life for which I'm eternally grateful.

**Estelle Condliff (Researcher) BBC Radio Merseyside.**

We all know how persuasive Bob could be. Never more so in my experience than when in January 1992, out of a clear blue sky, he convinced me that it would be a good idea to set off to Marrakesh to run in a half marathon there. Those who knew Bob will not be surprised to learn that it was not a package holiday he had in mind but a race against the clock, to make it in time for the run a couple of days hence. This involved a flight to Malaga, hiring a car there, then setting off on a breakneck journey, most of it in pitch darkness to reach Marrakesh for the run.

We passed through Algiers, Tenta, and then took a wrong road out of Rabat and crashed the car in a tiny isolated village. Bob's silver tongue enlisted the help of some locals who, although not enabling us to get to the race in time, joined us in a series of hair-raising adventures over the next couple of weeks.

In Metones one unforgettable conversation took place. A street trader asked Bob what he thought of "his beautiful country?" Bob said that he liked it, and the dialogue continued thus:

S.T. - "And what does your wife think of Morocco?"

Bob - "I've no idea. She's thousands.of miles away."

S.T. - (gesturing towards me) "No, your wife."

Now I am nearly six foot tall, 14 stones and have a face that only a mother could love. What a sad reflection on Moroccan women! Bob however, spent the rest of the trip referring to me as Mrs. Azurdia!

**Jim Callaway, Fairfield (fellow runner and personal friend).**

How long have I got? Mention Bob and memories come flooding back. When I first started at Radio Merseyside (circa 1977) he was a veritable font of knowledge - the greater the number of beers sunk in the pub next door after work, the more I marvelled at how much he knew about things many people would regard as inconsequential. Mention a sporting event and Bob could tell you which local athletes were taking part. Mention the Olympics or the Commonwealth Games and Bob had been there... his holidays had more to do with the organisational abilities of the IOC than ABTA. He treated everyone as equals and had time for everyone.

He also had the rare ability to wear jeans a lot of the time without a hint of disdain from management (how did he get away with it?). What you saw was what you got (never ever on time, I hasten to add!!!) But he was, quite simply, a one-off - a compassionate man, he was as unique as his surname.

**Roger Summerskill (Presenter) BBC Radio Merseyside.**

My wife Linda and I were very fond of Bob. Not only was he great company and a great raconteur but he was also a listener. Good listeners are rare and Bob made everybody feel that what they were saying was important.

I organised ten annual Scouseology media quiz nights. Radio Merseyside won nine of them! Bob, together with Liam Fogarty, had a wealth of diverse local knowledge few could match.

I still miss him.

**Phil Young (Merseyside Tourism and Conference Bureau)**

Bob Azurdia was a gentle man, a true friend and supporter of both local sport and sports people. His interest in and knowledge of international sporting events and achievements was immense and his radio programme "The Azurdia Interview" was a monumental piece of local radio.

However, perhaps Bob's greatest love was to take part in local road races and talk and provoke, like only he could, his fellow competitors as he ran the course - his presence, and support has, and will continue to be missed.

**From his friends at Liverpool City Council Leisure Services.**

***Ken Head and Bob covering the big game for Merseyside Hospital Radio***

Bob was both a close personal friend and colleague of mine for over 20 years. His professional approach to football commentating was without equal, and he made a valuable and irreplaceable contribution to the Merseyside Hospitals Radio Network. His convoluted messages on my answerphone were a joy to listen to. Bob's zest for life and his obvious enjoyment of everything he did has left an indelible mark on my life.

**Ken Head (Chairman) Merseyside Hospitals Radio Network.**

Bob was impossible. Impossibly good company, impossibly entertaining, impossibly laconic, impossibly irritating at times and impossibly knowledgeable on a bewildering assortment of obscurities.

It was impossible to have a five minute chat with Bob. It went on and on and - on until you were loosening your collar with exhaustion... or waving a white flag! I ran in many marathons and half marathons with Bob, together with Johnny Kennedy and Roger Lyon, but even the prospect of 26 miles 385 yards ahead of us couldn't silence Bob's incessant patter.

I recall one scorching hot race day at picturesque Lake Vyrnwy in North Wales. The stunning scenery, blistering 90 degree heat and the prospect of 13.2 miles ahead of us would be enough to render anyone speechless... but not Bob! As the sweat poured off us and the road ahead disappeared in a haze, Bob proffered theory after theory on everything from the virtues of masonry paint versus ordinary emulsion to the big bang theory.

Johnny and Roger were clearly more deft than I at edging ahead of Bob preferring silent concentration with only the odd word of encouragement exchanged. They merely grinned as they looked over their shoulder to see Bob in meaningful conversation with me as though we were lying prone on deckchairs with tequila in hand!

A half-cocked, dismissive answer was never good enough for Bob. He would ponder and challenge your every cursory word. But that was Bob. Anxious to share acquired knowledge and information and to live life to the full.

On my way to my mum's on a Saturday afternoon I would always see him scurrying along Anfield Road towards the football ground, with tape recorder over his shoulder, dressed in familiar short sleeved t-shirt and jeans whatever the weather and always late. I'd toot and he'd wave.

Once, when I got to the house and switched on Radio Merseyside to listen to match commentary I heard Bob say - "You join us here at Goodison in glorious sunshi*e...er, sunshine!"

That utterance and others, like his reaction when he was arrested live on air for causing an obstruction during the Pope's visit to Liverpool, have passed into legend. Just like him.

I have a picture on my wall of Bob, Johnny, Roger and me sitting on a sandstone wall at Lake Vyrnwy holding our hard won medals. Bob's the only one talking.

**Linda McDermott (Presenter) BBC Radio Merseyside.**

"Of course, you do know that the fifth horse in last years Grand National has Liverpool connections, don't you?"

"Yes, Bob".

You didn't but you knew that Bob knew you didn't. More importantly he knew you didn't. Not only did he have a wealth of knowledge and a point of view on matters that concerned him but he had a masterful way of making and starting a conversation... with anyone. Had there been an Olympic event called 'verbal fencing' then Bob would have won it hands down.

I can still see him elegantly holding down his grey beard so as not to have it swimming like a redundant ferret in, his pint of best bitter.... waiting for a moment in the conversation which would allow him to steer it in to the next half hour... just when you thought it was time to head home!

My first memory of Bob was as a new boy at Radio Merseyside and seeing him dashing into the office, grabbing his huge pile of albums and scurrying out again five seconds flat as the theme to his afternoon show was playing in the studio a floor above having been started by the previous presenter with Bob nowhere to be seen…and then taking the level of his voice 'off air' with a phrase that had something to do with his dog!

He always made it in time and would glide through the next three hours as if he'd been preparing for hours before. To say he was a character is an understatement in the extreme.

**Alan Jackson (Presenter) BBC Radio Merseyside.**

"Do you know how to use a tape recorder?...." "No, I don't" What about editing tape, making a package?" "No, I'm afraid I don't" "Oh" says Bob, "Well I'd better show you"

That was only my second week working with Radio Merseyside and Bob took me under his wing and taught me about interviewing, recording and much, much more. He was always supportive, encouraging and caring. He always had time for people, and always brought out the best in them.

His sense of humour was at times wicked, but always witty. Bob was one of life's gentlemen... and someone who I learnt so much from about broadcasting and life. I will always value and treasure his influence.

**Angela Heslop (Presenter) BBC Radio Merseyside.**

Bob Azurdia was a broadcasting legend. Not for him the glory of national radio, but the intimate style of a local station.

I think he was the most interesting man I've ever talked to. Music, the arts, travel and of course his first love sport, he could talk for hours on most subjects and often did. You only struck up a conversation with Bob if you desperately needed to know a fact from his vast encyclopaedia mind, or had half an hour to kill. There are so many stories about Bob, some true, some false and some exaggerated as they so often are about favourite characters.

I still look for him in the press box and he's probably still there in some form.

**Roger Hughes (Sports Broadcaster) BBC Radio Merseyside.**

I had a friendship with Bob from when I first met him, in as much as his father was my parent's doctor. Throughout my long career at Liverpool, Bob was always there. I regarded him as a very talented man who always got the best out of you in interviews by building up a trust btween you. I was lucky enough to carry on our relationship after my playing days and, right up to his death, I regarded myself as a good friend of both him and Mariuccia. We mixed in the same social circle and I always looked forward to seeing him. He was a true character - an 'oddball' in the loveliest sense and a person I genuinely liked to be with. He was undoubtedly eccentric and great company. I miss him very much..

**Ian Callaghan - ex-Liverpool Football Club**

Where Bob Azurdia is concerned, it's difficult to know where to start... but one particular memory is frequently rekindled in my mind.

It was a night game at Prenton Park, home of Tranmere Rovers. I was, at that time, a raw novice in the radio business, and it was one of the first matches I was ever trusted to cover. Being a beginner, I wasn't doing commentary but was asked to do some "off air" commentary, just in case some goals were scored... it's also a good way of honing your skills.

It meant there was a spare seat next to me in the press box...and as the match was progressing, I could see Bob walking across in my direction - he rarely arrived in time for the kick off!

To be honest, I was desperately hoping he wouldn't sit next to me. I didn't want him to hear all my mistakes. I knew I was in ear shot of a radio legend and my nervous system began to take a battering.

But, unusually, Bob said nothing...until half time. He said I was doing well and even apologised for offering some advice but that advice has stayed with me to this day. He told me to "paint pictures", to be the eyes of the listener, to avoid being too descriptive and, above all, mention the colours: the team shirts, the terraces, even the sky. It sounds obvious but, thinking about it, I realised I wasn't doing any of these things!

It was a valuable lesson and I was so pleased he'd found the time to point it out to me - but that was Bob, always a kind word for those starting out. A rare quality indeed.

**Ian Kennedy (Sports Reporter) BBC Radio Merseyside.**

The scene: a curry house in Liverpool, every Friday night in the late '60's about llpm. The case: Bob - and sundry friends and colleagues.

We would eat. Bob would talk, wonderful tales of his travels. My favourite was of Fat Abdul who sat in the square in Tangier. Bob would finish his rice. He'd order more. His curry would run out. He'd ask for more. Still he'd talk...until curry, rice, stories and the patience of the Indian waiters was exhausted.

I'll never forget Fat Abdul. Or Bob

**Jenny Collins, BBC Radio Merseyside**

In the 1970's I was the Hon Secretary of the Liverpool Football Coaching Association which was actively involved in promoting football all over Merseyside. With the co-operation and help of the Liverpool Parks and Gardens Department, we used to organise coaching sessions for school children at various venues around the city for several weeks during the summer holidays. Each venue held a 5-a-side competitions for different age groups, the winners of which went on to a final stage at the old Liverpool Show at Wavertree Playground.

On the evening of the finals one year, although we had plenty of coaches there to organise things, for one reason or another we didn't have a well known personality to present the prizes to the winners.

Then I spotted Bob, one of our vice-presidents in the crowd and although he had been about to go home he readily agreed to stay on and present the medals for us. One little lad came forward with his dad to receive his medal and looked open-mouthed at Bob. His dad bent down and in a stage-whisper said "You know who this is, don't yer? It's 'im off the wireless, Bomber Zodiac."

"Bomber Zodiac" as I will always remember him, was a generous, kindly man and the L.F.C.A. were privileged to have him as a Vice President. It's perhaps fitting that the nature of his passing was during an event to help others less fortunate than he.

**Peter Rutherford (a listener).**

I first met Bob in 1983 when he ran in the first Speke 10k Boxing Day Race, some 500 runners turning up to raise money for the "Bone Marrow Appeal" at the

Royal Liverpool Hospital. £1,000 was raised.

During 1984, running myself, I bumped into Bob at most local races and fun runs. At the time, the Speke 10k committee was looking for an honorary president. Having met and got to know Bob and his own fund raising activities, we invited him to become our Hon. president of the Speke 10k committee.

During Bob's time with us, he encouraged us no end, offering ideas he had picked up from the many races he had run around the world. One of the ideas was that Bob reckoned that most races organisers started races at least 15 minutes early - it took us a while to realise that Bob always arrived just before the gun went off. Another reason would be 'last in the car park, first out', but in Bob's case, that did not work either because he always stayed behind for a chat and a pint. Bob would always be in the last quarter of the race to finish but in hail, rain or snow, he would stand at the end and applaud in the back markers of the race, shivering in his infamous Radio Merseyside running vest.

In Helsby, in January 1996, I saw Bob running in to finish his last half marathon, sporting his running vest. Ron Hart and I decided to wait for Bob at the bar of the BICC club. We heard the ambulance leaving the finish area, unaware that Bob was on his way to hospital, having collapsed whilst crossing the finishing line.

An Olympic Torch was commissioned by John Moores University through Charles Lambert to celebrate 100 years, 1896 - 1996. We were given permission to add to above dates, "Bob Azurdia, 1935 - 1996". The torch will become the British Olympic Torch and will be handed over to the British Olympic Committee. Bob used to say, "It wasn't the winning, but the taking part."

You certainly took part in the race of life, Bob, and will be missed by all your running friends on Merseyside and around the world.

Rest in peace, Bob.

**Jim Ross (Chairman) Speke IOk Committee.**

***Terry Waite being interviewed after his release from captivity.***

As one of the many charities that benefited from Bob's enthusiasm and commitment, we were saddened by his sudden death. However, the manner of his going would, I am sure, be one in which Bob would have been pleased, not for him asleep in bed but rather at the end of a difficult and hard race. Bob's commitment to charities on Merseyside will be sadly missed but the memory of his enthusiasm is one that still brings a smile to all of our faces.

**Stephen Yip (Founder) Kids in Need and Distress (KIND).**

Soon after getting a job at Radio Merseyside, I turned up for an early shift at about five in the morning. Fast asleep across a row of chairs in the small reception area was my new colleague Bob Azurdia. There was a note pinned to his pullover. On it, he'd written: "I'm on earlies. Please wake me when you arrive." It struck me then that here was a one-off. I was right. To say that you ever came upon anybody like Bob Azurdia is like saying you're bored by the company of extra terrestrials.

**Dick Duckenfield (former Manager) BBC Radio Merseyside.**

I always think of Bob in the present tense. It is difficult to write of him as though he has gone. He was a person in love with the immediate: the "Now". So he was a natural pioneer. Yet he also possessed an unflinching sense of history. He would enjoy a good story yet it would never be allowed to remain in the past; it would need to have some impact upon the present. His friendship with the prime "movers and shakers" of Merseyside public life over many years made the place seem like a village in his company. His pioneering spirit helped create BBC local radio at the outset when there were no blueprints. His natural, yet relentlessly questioning faith, I always found refreshing. Like the best mentors, he taught through his friendship - and I thank God for him.

**Steve Williams (Religious Affairs Producer) BBC Radio Merseyside (a job that Bob first held and created from nothing in 1967)**

***Two jazz greats! Bob poses with his all-time favourite performer Louis Armstrong***

I first met Bob in 1980. I was ambitious to become a Radio Presenter and rang Radio Merseyside to ask for some information on how best to go about it. I was put through to Bob who could not have been more helpful.

He arranged to take me, a total stranger, to one of his many watering holes, bought me a drink and spent the next several hours telling me of all the benefits and pitfalls of the radio industry - and particularly the BBC. His advice was "never give up", and although it took five years, I did eventually manage to present my own show on Radio Merseyside.

The great thing about Bob Azurdia was that he had time for anyone and everyone.

**Debi Jones (former Radio Merseyside presenter).**

Bob Azurdia was a perfectionist and I experienced this side of his character first hand. Bob asked me to take part in a special documentary programme he was making about VE Day and VJ Day anniversaries.

He wanted a journalist from the Liverpool Echo of the '90's to read out the stories and reports from his own personal collection of our war time editions. Knowing him both professionally and socially, I knew he would put his usual endless energies into the project.

At the time however, I was suffering from a poisoned finger which was very painful and I had made an appointment to see a specialist. I told Bob I could spare about 40 minutes. That agreed, we went into the studio at BBC Radio Merseyside: "It will be wrapped up within an hour," he said cheerily, scratching his beard. Bob brought in his original Echoes - yellowed and tattered and real museum pieces. He stood staring at them while proudly proclaiming them to be his "pride and joy."

Four hours later, I emerged from the studio exhausted, in agony and having missed my appointment and with a five hour hospital wait in casualty beckoning. It was all worth it.

When I heard the final broadcast it was faultless. A testament to a man who had a healthy obsession with getting things right.

**Peter Grant (Television and Radio Editor) Liverpool Echo.**

During his time on Earth, Bob interviewed just about everyone from Mother Theresa to his local refuse collector. Just imagine the infinite list of historical figures that he now has at his disposal to be his "victims". I can just close my eyes and envisage the "Celestial Azurdia Interview" with the likes of Napoleon, H G Wells, Gallileo, Julius Caesar, Jessie Owens or Adolph Hitler!

One thing is certain, whoever was on the other side of the microphone, they wouldn't get the better of Bob!

Thoughts of Bob are seldom far away and I find him very therapeutic. No matter what mood I may be in at any given time, I only have to focus my mind on the bristling beard, the twinkling eyes and wiggling ears (a party piece of his) and it is guaranteed to bring a smile to my face. He was many things to many people but to me he was simply "my mate Bob."

**Roger Lyon**